Measureme

Geometry by Design

Second Edition

Russell F. Jacobs

Jacobs Publishing
An imprint of Tessellations

Phoenix, Arizona

AUTHOR: Russell F. Jacobs

The author wishes to credit Patricia Wright for the "search n shade" concept used in *Measurement and Geometry by Design*. She introduced this idea in her *Search n Shade* and *Compute a Design* books, also published by Jacobs Publishing.

Contributor to the Second Edition: Robert Fathauer

Editorial Assistants: Erika Jacobs, Janette Smidt, Gabriel Lucero, Jr. and Neil McConnell

Note on the second edition: The final four exercises, new to this edition, were written by Robert Fathauer. The first 40 exercises, which were in the first edition, were written by Russell F. Jacobs.

To the Teacher:

The following directions may be helpful in getting students started with *Measurement and Geometry by Design*.

"Work each exercise. Then search for the answer on the grid. Each answer will appear one or more times. Shade each polygon containing the answer just like the small polygon next to the exercise is shaded. If the grid is shaded correctly, a pleasing design emerges."

Both the student and the teacher usually can tell at once if the work is not correct. Most of the designs are symmetrical. Any errors in working the exercises or in shading are noticeable. For convenience, an Answer Key for all the activities is included in the back of the book. Some useful tables are also included in the back of the book. These include a Table of Sines, Cosines, and Tangents; a Table of Squares; a Table of Metric and Customary Measures; and a Table of Metric/Customary Approximate Equivalents. You will want to duplicate these pages of tables for students to use in working related exercises.

Some students will want to create some artistically elegant designs in color. It is recommended that they first do the shading in pencil to make sure the design is correct. Then they can redo the design in color on a separate grid using a color felt pen.

The exercises in *Measurement and Geometry by Design* are for review and practice of certain skills and concepts. In exercises involving solution of equations, to avoid guessing of answers, you will probably want students to show the steps of solving each equation. In exercises involving word problems, you will probably want students to write an equation for each problem and show the steps in solving each equation.

ISBN 978-0-9846042-1-0

Table of Contents

ACTIVITY 1

Name _____

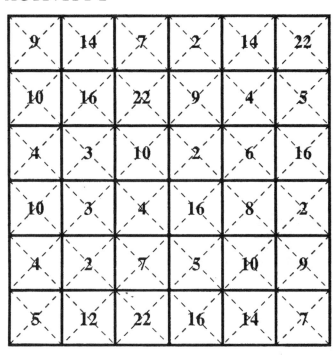

Find each length to the nearest whole unit.

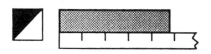

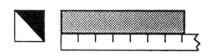

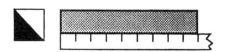

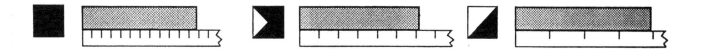

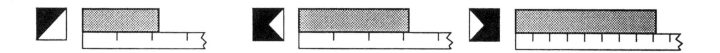

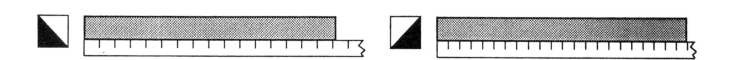

ACTIVITY 2

Name _____

$\frac{12}{10}$	1	$\frac{7}{5}$	$\frac{7}{5}$	$\frac{43}{8}$	$\frac{5}{4}$
$\frac{9}{4}$	$\frac{12}{10}$	$\frac{10}{2}$	$\frac{10}{2}$	$\frac{5}{4}$	$\frac{5}{2}$
3	$\frac{15}{12}$	$\frac{15}{8}$	$\frac{15}{8}$	$\frac{4}{3}$	$\frac{8}{6}$
3	$\frac{15}{12}$	$\frac{15}{8}$	$\frac{15}{8}$	$\frac{4}{3}$	$\frac{8}{6}$
$\frac{5}{4}$	$\frac{43}{8}$	$\frac{19}{4}$	$\frac{19}{4}$	1	$\frac{12}{10}$
$\frac{5}{2}$	$\frac{5}{4}$	$\frac{22}{8}$	$\frac{22}{8}$	$\frac{12}{10}$	$\frac{9}{4}$

Find each length, using the unit indicated.

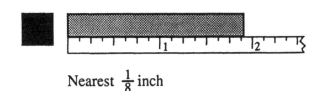

Nearest $\frac{1}{8}$ inch

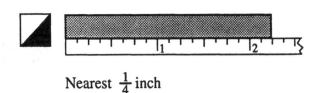

Nearest $\frac{1}{4}$ inch

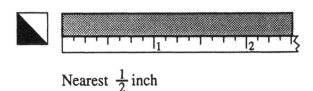

Nearest $\frac{1}{2}$ inch

Nearest inch

Nearest $\frac{1}{6}$ inch

Nearest $\frac{1}{12}$ inch

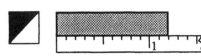

Nearest $\frac{1}{10}$ inch

Nearest $\frac{1}{5}$ inch

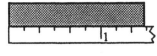

Nearest $\frac{1}{3}$ inch

Write the measurement at each point using the nearest unit given.

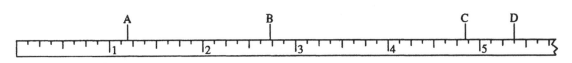

 A, $\frac{1}{4}$-inch

 B, 1-inch

 C, $\frac{1}{2}$-inch

 D, $\frac{1}{8}$-inch

 B, $\frac{1}{8}$-inch

 C, $\frac{1}{4}$-inch

Measurement and Geometry by Design / Russell F. Jacobs   www.tessellations.com   © 1997 Jacobs Publishing Company

ACTIVITY 3

Name _____

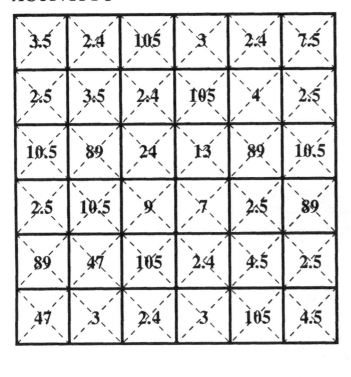

Find each length, using the unit indicated.

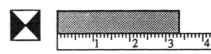

Nearest centimeter

Nearest 0.5 centimeter

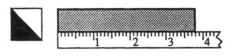

Nearest centimeter

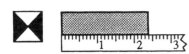

Nearest 0.1 centimeter

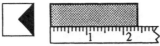

Nearest millimeter

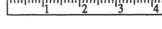

Nearest 0.5 centimeter

Find the measurement at each point, using the unit indicated.

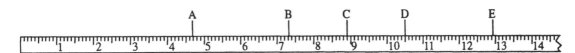

 A, 0.5-cm   B, 1-cm   C, 1-mm

 D, 1-mm   E, 1-cm   A, 1-mm

 B, 0.5-cm   C, 1-cm   D, 0.5-cm

Measurement and Geometry by Design / Russell F. Jacobs   www.tessellations.com   © 1997 Jacobs Publishing Company

ACTIVITY 4

Name _____

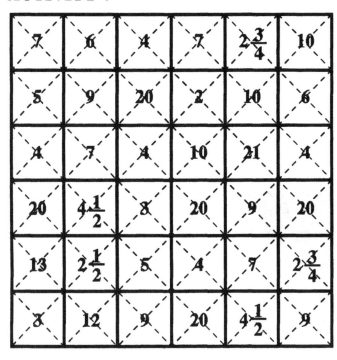

Find the number of feet represented by each measurement.

 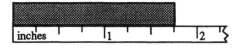

Scale: $\frac{1}{4}$-inch = 1 foot

 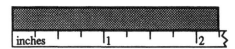

Scale: $\frac{3}{4}$-inch = 1 foot

Scale: $\frac{1}{8}$-inch = 1 foot

 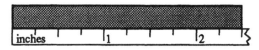

Scale: $\frac{1}{2}$-inch = 1 foot

 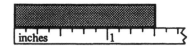

Scale: $\frac{3}{8}$-inch = 1 foot

 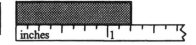

Scale: $\frac{5}{8}$-inch = 1 foot

A, Scale: $\frac{1}{8}$-inch = 1 foot

B, Scale: $\frac{1}{4}$-inch = 1 foot

C, Scale: 1-inch = 1 foot

D, Scale: $\frac{1}{2}$-inch = 1 foot

E, Scale: $\frac{3}{8}$-inch = 1 foot

F, Scale: $\frac{1}{4}$-inch = 1 foot

G, Scale: $\frac{3}{4}$-inch = 1 foot

H, Scale: $1\frac{1}{2}$-inch = 1 foot

I, Scale: $1\frac{1}{4}$-inch = 1 foot

ACTIVITY 5

Name _____

12 rd 2 yd	6 yd 30 in	9 yd 11 in	9 yd 11 in	1 ft 5 in	9 yd 4 in
9 rd 1 ft	8 ft 1 in	3 rd 10 ft	6 yd 1 ft	9 yd 4 in	9 rd 1 ft
1 yd 2 ft	1 ft 10 in	12 rd 2 yd	9 yd 4 in	7 rd 2 yd	2 yd 2 in
1 yd 2 ft	9 yd 4 in	6 yd 1 ft	1 ft 10 in	8 ft 1 in	2 yd 2 in
17 yd 4 ft	7 rd 2 yd	9 yd 4 in	12 rd 2 yd	3 rd 10 ft	17 yd 4 ft
6 yd 1 ft	6 yd 30 in	2 ft 7 in	2 ft 7 in	1 ft 5 in	1 ft 10 in

Add or subtract. Simplify.

◢
5 ft 4 in
+ 2 ft 9 in
_____

◤
4 ft 3 in
− 2 ft 5 in
_____

◺
3 yd 2 ft
+ 2 yd 2 ft
_____

◣
3 yd 10 in
+ 5 yd 30 in
_____

▶
7 yd 1 ft
− 5 yd 2 ft
_____

◥
6 yd 15 in
− 5 yd 20 in
_____

◀
3 ft $5\frac{1}{4}$ in
+ 2 ft $8\frac{3}{4}$ in
_____

▼
4 yd $3\frac{1}{2}$ in
+ 5 yd $7\frac{1}{2}$ in
_____

◁
5 ft $1\frac{1}{2}$ in
− 3 ft $8\frac{1}{2}$ in
_____

▷
10 yd $2\frac{1}{4}$ in
− 3 yd $8\frac{1}{4}$ in
_____

▲
11 yd 37 in
+ 6 yd 11 in
_____

▽
6 rd 10 ft
+ 2 rd $7\frac{1}{2}$ ft
_____

◢
8 rd $3\frac{1}{2}$ yd
+ 3 rd 4 yd
_____

◤
10 rd 15 ft
− 7 rd 5 ft
_____

◸
25 rd 3 yd
− 18 rd 1 yd
_____

Measurement and Geometry by Design / Russell F. Jacobs   www.tessellations.com   © 1997 Jacobs Publishing Company

ACTIVITY 6

Name _____

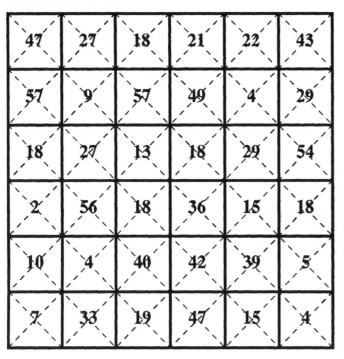

Select the unit that is best for each measurement.

 Width of a book cover
1. meter
2. millimeter
3. kilometer
4. centimeter

 Width of a small paper clip
5. millimeter
6. centimeter
7. meter
8. kilometer

 Distance between New York and Boston
9. meter
10. kilometer
11. centimeter
12. millimeter

 Width of camera film
13. inch
14. foot
15. millimeter
16. centimeter

 Length of an Olympic swim event
17. centimeter
18. meter
19. kilometer
20. foot

 Length of a ball-point pen
21. meter
22. centimeter
23. millimeter
24. foot

 Height of a tall building
25. millimeter
26. centimeter
27. meter
28. kilometer

 Weight of an adult person
29. kilogram
30. gram
31. ounce
32. liter

 Weight of a paper clip
33. gram
34. kilogram
35. pound
36. ounce

 Capacity of an auto fuel tank
37. milliliter
38. kiloliter
39. pint
40. liter

 Length of a marathon race
41. meter
42. kilometer
43. yard
44. foot

 Height of a mountain
45. mile
46. centimeter
47. meter
48. millimeter

 Capacity of a water glass
49. milliliter
50. gallon
51. quart
52. liter

 Width of a TV screen
53. meter
54. foot
55. millimeter
56. centimeter

 Length of a swimming pool
57. meter
58. kilometer
59. centimeter
60. inch

ACTIVITY 7

Name _____

3.40	40	72	3.4	2	4
34	6	3	14	60	8
2,000	0.25	340	72	34	20
2.5	200	60	72	2,000	0.25
30	72	3.4	2	2.5	200
6	3	14	340	600	72

Find the missing numbers.

 10, 560 ft = _?_ mi

 5,280 yd = _?_ mi

 72 in = _?_ ft

 5 ft = _?_ in   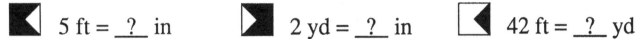 2 yd = _?_ in   42 ft = _?_ yd

12 ft = _?_ yd   2 km = _?_ m   3,400 m = _?_ km

3,400 cm = _?_ m   25 mm = _?_ cm   3,400 mm = _?_ cm

2 m = _?_ cm   2 cm = _?_ mm   25 cm = _?_ m

Measurement and Geometry by Design / Russell F. Jacobs   www.tessellations.com   © 1997 Jacobs Publishing Company

ACTIVITY 8

Name _____

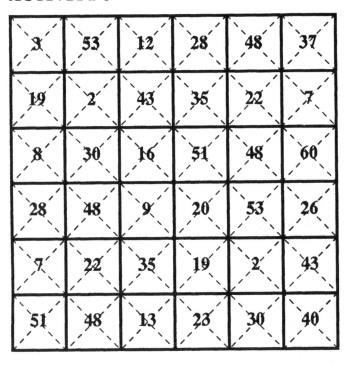

Select the measure that is closest in value to the given measure.

 100 meters
1. 1,000 in
2. 109 yd
3. 250 ft
4. $\frac{1}{4}$ mile

 24 liters
5. 24 gal
6. 30 pt
7. 25 qt
8. 200 c

 10 inches
9. 25 cm
10. 100 mm
11. 0.5 m
12. 40 cm

 5 kilometers
13. 3 mi
14. 500 m
15. 1,500 yd
16. 8 mi

 50 yards
17. 0.1 mi
18. 16.7 ft
19. 45 m
20. 0.45 km

 2 miles
21. 300 yd
22. 3.2 km
23. 2,500 m
24. 2,000 ft

 5 gallons
25. 2 kg
26. 20ℓ
27. 2 kℓ
28. 19ℓ

 4 kilograms
29. 400 g
30. 9 lb
31. 40ℓ
32. 100 oz

 10 ounces
33. 0.35 g
34. 10,000 kg
35. 283 g
36. 0.5 lb

 25 inches
37. 0.625 m
38. 250 mm
39. 22.5 cm
40. 1.44 yd

 24 pints
41. 1,140 kℓ
42. 6 kg
43. 11.4ℓ
44. 48 qt

 2,500 ft
45. 250 m
46. 7,500 cm
47. 75 yd
48. 0.75 km

 120 centimeters
49. 60 in
50. 1.2 kg
51. 4 ft
52. 15 yd

 44 pounds
53. 20 kg
54. 15,000 g
55. 2.75 oz
56. 96.8 kg

 800 milliliters
57. 850 qt
58. 8ℓ
59. 2 gal
60. 0.85 qt

Measurement and Geometry by Design / Russell F. Jacobs   www.tessellations.com   © 1997 Jacobs Publishing Company

ACTIVITY 9

Name _____

7,200	8	4	10,800	6	7,200
1,500	3	1,200	0.5	2.5	300
300	6	40	1,440	8	1,500
0.5	10,800	1,440	40	4	1,200
1,200	1	1,500	300	72	0.5
7,200	4	8	6	10,800	7,200

Find the missing numbers.

▼ 240 mi/hr =
___?___ mi/min

◀ 20 ft/sec =
___?___ ft/min

▲ 360 yd/min =
___?___ yd/sec

◸ 180 ft/min =
___?___ ft/sec

▶ 1,800 mi/hr =
___?___ mi/sec

■ 2 ft/sec =
___?___ ft/hr

◸ 24 yd/min =
___?___ ft/min

▲ 96 in/sec =
___?___ ft/sec

⊠ 2 ft/sec =
___?___ in/min

◺ 60 km/hr =
___?___ km/min

◀ 25 m/min =
___?___ m/hr

⊠ 4 cm/sec =
___?___ mm/sec

◣ 25 mm/min =
___?___ cm/min

▼ 3 cm/sec =
___?___ cm/hr

▶ 50 mm/sec =
___?___ cm/min

Measurement and Geometry by Design / Russell F. Jacobs   www.tessellations.com   © 1997 Jacobs Publishing Company

Name _____

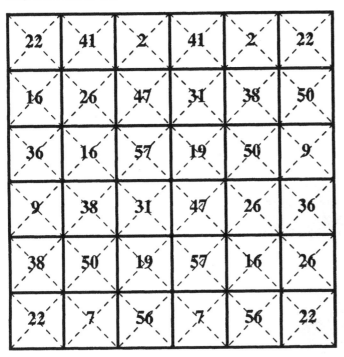

Select the measure that is the best choice in each exercise.

 Width of a sheet of paper
1. 17 cm
2. 8.5 in
3. 200 mm
4. 0.9 ft

 Capacity of a can of soda
5. 1 pt
6. 0.5 *l*
7. 355 m*l*
8. 16 oz

 Speed limit in a school zone
9. 15 mi/hr
10. 100 yd/min
11. 50 ft/sec
12. 3 mi/hr

 Mass (weight) of a newborn baby
13. 7 kg
14. 350 g
15. 250 m*l*
16. 128 oz

 Height of the Washington Monument
17. 75 m
18. 0.5 mi
19. 550 ft
20. 0.75 km

 Size of a TV screen
21. 3.5 ft
22. 26 in
23. 100 cm
24. 200 mm

 Width of camera film
25. 1.75 in
26. 35 mm
27. 4.3 cm
28. 0.35 m

 Capacity of an auto's gas tank
29. 48 pt
30. 200 m*l*
31. 45 *l*
32. 120 qt

 Cruising speed of a passenger jet
33. 1,000 ft/sec
34. 150 km/hr
35. 400 m/min
36. 7.5 mi/min

 Average height of a women's basketball team
37. 2.3 m
38. 71 in
39. 250 cm
40. 800 mm

 High speed of a commuter train
41. 120 km/hr
42. 5 mi/min
43. 300 m/min
44. 35 mi/hr

 Length of a woman's shoe
45. 50 cm
46. 1.2 ft
47. 10 in
48. 175 mm

 Capacity of a water glass
49. 500 m*l*
50. 1 cup
51. 0.25 *l*
52. 400 g

 Length of a new pencil
53. 10 in
54. 150 mm
55. 0.3 m
56. 19 cm

 Size of a computer diskette
57. 3.5 in
58. 5 cm
59. 125 mm
60. 0.5 kg

www.tessellations.com

ACTIVITY 11

Name _____

9 wk 1 day	7 yr 4 mo	8 hr 30 min	6 hr 5 min	5 hr 51 sec	6 hr 1 min
6 hr 45 min	3 min 13 sec	8 hr 9 min	4 wk 5 da	6 hr 1 sec	6 wk 2 da
6 hr 1 min	6 da 3 hr	5 wk 5 hr	8 hr 30 min	4 yr 7 mo	9 wk 1 day
6 hr 5 min	5 hr 51 sec	6 hr 1 min	22 min 6 sec	7 yr 4 mo	8 hr 30 min
4 wk 5 da	7 hr 9 min	6 wk 2 da	6 hr 45 min	3 min 13 sec	8 hr 9 min
8 hr 30 min	4 yr 7 mo	22 min 6 sec	6 hr 1 min	6 da 3 hr	6 hr 5 min

Add or Subtract. Simplify.

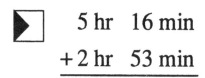

$$5 \text{ hr} \quad 16 \text{ min}$$
$$+\,2 \text{ hr} \quad 53 \text{ min}$$

$$12 \text{ min} \quad 25 \text{ sec}$$
$$-\,9 \text{ min} \quad 12 \text{ sec}$$

$$3 \text{ wk} \quad 5 \text{ da}$$
$$+\,2 \text{ wk} \quad 4 \text{ da}$$

$$10 \text{ hr} \quad 5 \text{ min}$$
$$-\,3 \text{ hr} \quad 20 \text{ min}$$

$$4 \text{ yr} \quad 7 \text{ mo}$$
$$+\,2 \text{ yr} \quad 9 \text{ mo}$$

$$2 \text{ da} \quad 15 \text{ hr}$$
$$+\,3 \text{ da} \quad 12 \text{ hr}$$

$$7 \text{ wk} \quad 5 \text{ da}$$
$$-\,2 \text{ wk} \quad 7 \text{ da}$$

$$3 \text{ hr} \quad 15 \text{ min}$$
$$+\,2 \text{ hr} \quad 50 \text{ min}$$

$$5 \text{ wk} \quad 3 \text{ hr}$$
$$+\,4 \text{ wk} \quad 21 \text{ hr}$$

$$10 \text{ yr} \quad 3 \text{ mo}$$
$$-\,5 \text{ yr} \quad 8 \text{ mo}$$

$$14 \text{ min} \quad 17 \text{ sec}$$
$$+\,7 \text{ min} \quad 49 \text{ sec}$$

$$12 \text{ hr} \quad 10 \text{ min}$$
$$-\,3 \text{ hr} \quad 40 \text{ min}$$

$$3 \text{ hr} \quad 23 \text{ sec}$$
$$+\,2 \text{ hr} \quad 28 \text{ sec}$$

$$10 \text{ wk} \quad 13 \text{ hr}$$
$$-\,5 \text{ wk} \quad 8 \text{ hr}$$

$$2 \text{ hr} \quad 13 \text{ sec}$$
$$+\,4 \text{ hr} \quad 47 \text{ sec}$$

ACTIVITY 12

Name _____

336	104	14	180	72	1
4	180	5	48	336	4
6	72	9	14	5	240
9	5	3	240	104	336
48	6	4	5	1	36
180	2	1	3	72	6

Find the missing numbers.

2 wk = __?__ da

36 mo = __?__ yr

120 sec = __?__ min

2 da = __?__ hr

240 min = __?__ hr

3 min = __?__ sec

2 yr = __?__ wk

120 hr = __?__ da

3,600 sec = __?__ hr

63 da = __?__ wk

2 wk = __?__ hr

3 yr = __?__ mo

4 hr = __?__ min

3 da = __?__ hr

312 wk = __?__ yr

ACTIVITY 13

Name _____

12:30	8:30	9:00	1:30	2:30	10:00
2:30	5:00	8:30	4:00	10:00	8:00
7:00	11:00	10:00	12:30	2:00	3:30
3:00	9:00	12:30	5:00	1:30	6:00
4:00	10:00	8:00	2:30	12:30	8:00
5:00	8:30	11:00	7:00	4:00	5:00

The mainland of the United States covers four time zones shown below. The corresponding time in Anchorage, Alaska, is 2:00. The corresponding time in Honolulu, Hawaii, is 1:00. In the summer, most states use Daylight Saving Time. Clocks in states with D.S.T. are set one hour later than standard time for that zone.

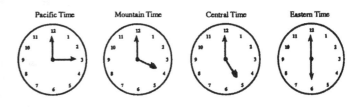

Refer to the information shown above.
Find the missing time.

 4:00 p.m. in Denver
_?_ p.m. in Atlanta

 5:00 p.m. in Chicago
_?_ p.m. in Seattle

 3:00 p.m. in Los Angeles
_?_ p.m. in St. Louis

 1:00 p.m. in Honolulu
_?_ p.m. in Phoenix

 5:00 p.m. in Houston
_?_ p.m. in Anchorage

 1:30 p.m. in Portland
_?_ p.m. in New Orleans

 1:00 p.m. in Boston
_?_ a.m. in San Francisco

 9:00 a.m. D.S.T. in Miami
_?_ a.m. Standard Time in Miami

 11:30 p.m. D.S.T. in San Francisco
_?_ a.m. D.S.T. in Chicago

 5:30 p.m. D.S.T. in New York
_?_ p.m. Standard Time in Phoenix

 11:30 a.m. D.S.T. in Portland
_?_ a.m. Standard Time in Honolulu

 9:00 a.m. D.S.T. in Anchorage
_?_ a.m. Standard Time in Honolulu

 9:30 a.m. Standard Time in Seattle
_?_ p.m. Standard Time in Boston

 3:00 p.m. D.S.T. in Atlanta
_?_ a.m. D.S.T. in Anchorage

 5:00 a.m. Standard Time in Seattle
_?_ a.m. D.S.T. in New York

ACTIVITY 14

Name _____

1545	11:45 p.m.	12:45 a.m.	12:45 a.m.	1545	9:45 a.m.
7:45 p.m.	1145	11:45 a.m.	10:45 p.m.	8:45 p.m.	1745
12:45 p.m.	2145	1545	9:45 a.m.	2145	0145
0845	2145	7:45 p.m.	1745	2145	0145
1545	8:45 p.m.	10:45 p.m.	11:45 a.m.	1145	11:45 p.m.
7:45 p.m.	1745	6:45 a.m.	6:45 a.m.	7:45 p.m.	1745

The 24-hour time system is used by the armed forces and in many airline and train schedules.

Examples:

12-hour system	24-hour system
5:00 a.m.	0500
3:00 p.m.	1500
9:45 a.m.	0945
12:30 p.m.	1230

Add 12 to p.m. time 1:00 or more, to get 24-hour time.

Subtract 1200 from 24-hour time more than 1200 to get 12-hour p.m. time.

Change each time to the 24-hour system.

 8:45 a.m.   3:45 p.m.   1:45 a.m.

 5:45 p.m.   9:45 p.m.   11:45 a.m.

Change each time to the 12-hour system.

 2245   0045   0945

 1245   2045   0645

 2345    1145   1945

Measurement and Geometry by Design / Russell F. Jacobs   www.tessellations.com   © 1997 Jacobs Publishing Company

Name _____

10 lb 6 oz	1 pt 7 oz	3 qt 1 pt	3 qt 2 oz	1 gal 3 qt	9 gal 1 qt
2 qt 11 oz	1 gal 3 qt	1 gal 2 qt	11 lb 9 oz	1 pt 7 oz	1 qt 1 pt
5 gal 3 qt	1 lb 11 oz	8 gal 1 qt	2 qt 11 oz	3 qt 2 oz	1 c 5 oz
1 pt 1 c	11 lb 9 oz	1 pt 7 oz	1 qt 1 pt	5 gal 3 qt	1 pt 1 c
1 gal 3 qt	2 qt 11 oz	1 lb 11 oz	1 c 5 oz	10 lb 6 oz	1 pt 7 oz
9 gal 1 qt	1 qt 1 pt	3 qt 1 pt	1 gal 2 qt	2 qt 11 oz	8 gal 1 qt

Add or subtract. Simplify.

◣　2 gal 3 qt
　+5 gal 2 qt
　_____

◤　5 qt 1 pt
　−3 qt 2 pt
　_____

■　6 gal 1 pt
　+3 gal 1 pt
　_____

◣　4 qt 2 pt
　+1 qt 2 pt
　_____

▼　3 pt 1 c
　−1 pt 2 c
　_____

◀　2 qt 1 c
　+1 qt 1 c
　_____

◣　4 lb 10 oz
　+5 lb 12 oz
　_____

◢　6 lb 3 oz
　−4 lb 8 oz
　_____

▶　7 lb 15 oz
　+3 lb 10 oz
　_____

◥　1 c 3 oz
　+1 c 4 oz
　_____

▶　3 c 2 oz
　−1 c 5 oz
　_____

◢　2 pt 11 oz
　+3 pt 7 oz
　_____

◺　3 qt 1 pt
　−1 qt 5 oz
　_____

◀　3 gal 4 pt
　+2 gal 1 qt
　_____

▼　4 gal 1 pt
　−2 gal 5 pt
　_____

Name _____

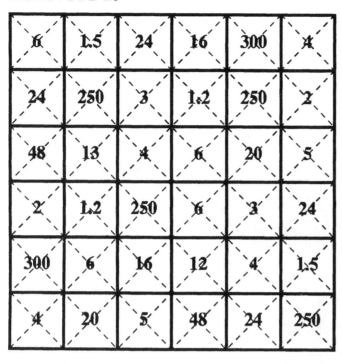

Find the missing numbers.

◻️ (white/black triangle) 3 lb = __?__ oz

◻️ (triangle) 3 gal = __?__ qt

◼️ 8 pt = __?__ qt

◻️ 2 gal = __?__ pt   ◼️ 96 oz = __?__ lb   ◻️ 52 qt = __?__ gal

◻️ 40 pt = __?__ gal   ◻️ 4,000 lb = __?__ T   ◼️ 0.25 kg = __?__ g

◻️ 1,500 ml = __?__ l   ◻️ 1,200 g = __?__ kg   ◻️ 5 qt = __?__ c

◼️ 12 qt = __?__ pt   ◻️ 48 c = __?__ gal   ◻️ 0.3 kl = __?__ l

ACTIVITY 17

Name _____

5	0.01	10	2,000	500	500
0.01	100	1	300	1,000	1,000
10	2,000	0.001	30	300	2,000
1	10	30	0.001	1	10
50	50	300	2,000	3,000	0.1
0.3	0.3	1	10	0.1	3,000

Find the missing numbers.

■   1 g = _?_ kg

⊠   1 ℓ = _?_ dℓ

⊠   10 mℓ = _?_ cℓ

◨   1 dℓ = _?_ ℓ   � 1 kℓ = _?_ ℓ   ◹ 1ℓ = _?_ cℓ

◸   10 g = _?_ kg   ⊠ 2 kg = _?_ g   ◲ 5 cℓ = _?_ mℓ

◿   5 g = _?_ cg   ◸ 0.5 kℓ = _?_ hℓ   ◪ 3 g = _?_ mg

◺   3 g = _?_ dkg   ■ 3 kg = _?_ hg   ⊠ 3 dℓ = _?_ mℓ

ACTIVITY 18

Name _____

104°	80°	– 20°	15°	100°	50°
– 10°	5°	14°	95°	104°	7°
23°	113°	68°	20°	41°	30°
95°	15°	10°	77°	– 20°	14°
40°	104°	30°	23°	5°	60°
50°	110°	41°	113°	4°	104°

Here is the formula for converting Celsius degrees to Fahrenheit degrees.

$$F = 1.8C + 32$$

If C = 0, then F = 32.

Use this formula to convert Fahrenheit degrees to Celsius degrees.

$$C = \frac{5}{9}(F - 32)$$

If F = 212, then C = 100.

20° C = __?__ F   5° C = __?__ F   25° C = __?__ F

40° C = __?__ F   35° C = __?__ F   45° C = __?__ F

50° F = __?__ C   59° F = __?__ C   41° F = __?__ C

68° F = __?__ C   122° F = __?__ C   86° F = __?__ C

– 5° C = __?__ F   – 10° C = __?__ F   – 4° F = __?__ C

Measurement and Geometry by Design / Russell F. Jacobs   www.tessellations.com

ACTIVITY 19

Name _____

12	10	24	6	27	9
4	12	2	15	9	4
3	6	20	20	24	8
15	6	126	126	24	2
16	5	3	3	60	16
5	10	24	6	27	60

Refer to the Table of Special Measures.

2 fathoms = __?__ ft

5 leagues = __?__ mi

24 furlongs = __?__ mi

2 hogsheads = __?__ gal

15 hands = __?__ in

3 firkins = __?__ gal

8 pecks = __?__ bushels

2,640 ft = __?__ furlongs

36 ft = __?__ fathoms

81 gal = __?__ firkins

5 bushels = __?__ pecks

64 in = __?__ hands

30 mi = __?__ leagues

3 mi = __?__ furlongs

600 ft = __?__ bolts

Measurement and Geometry by Design / Russell F. Jacobs   www.tessellations.com   © 1997 Jacobs Publishing Company

ACTIVITY 20

Name _____

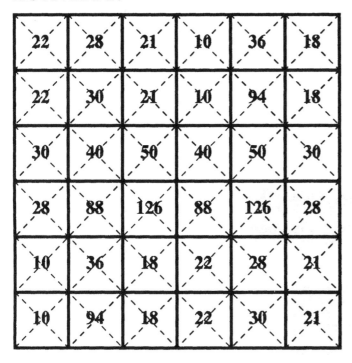

Here is the formula for the perimeter of a rectangle.

$$P = 2(\text{Length} + \text{Width})$$

W = 3 in

L = 5 in

$$P = 2(5 + 3)$$
$$P = 2(8)$$
$$P = 16 \text{ in}$$

Find the perimeter of each rectangle.

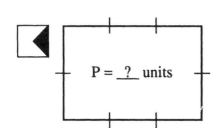

P = _?_ units

 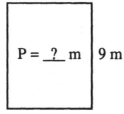

P = _?_ m   9 m

5 m

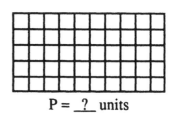

P = _?_ units

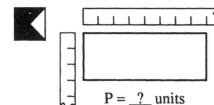

P = _?_ units

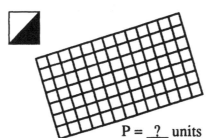

P = _?_ units

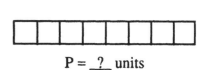

P = _?_ units

 Length = 35 ft
Width = 12 ft
Perimeter = _?_ ft

Length = 42 mm
Width = 21 mm
Perimeter = _?_ mm

 Length = 24 cm
Width = 20 cm
Perimeter = _?_ cm

Find each missing measure for a rectangle.

 Perimeter = 120 mm
Width = 24 mm
Length = _?_ mm

 Perimeter = 78 cm
Width = 18 cm
Length = _?_ cm

 Perimeter = 100 m
Sum of Length
and Width = _?_ cm

Name _____

20	36	44	20	44	6
10	28	6	10	108	50
44	6	20	6	10	20
10	20	44	10	44	6
165	62	20	44	8	20
44	6	10	6	144	10

Here is the formula for the area of a rectangle.

$$A = (Length)(Width)$$

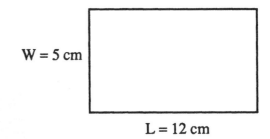

W = 5 cm

L = 12 cm

$$A = (12)(5)$$

$$A = 60 \text{ cm}^2$$

Find the area of each rectangle.

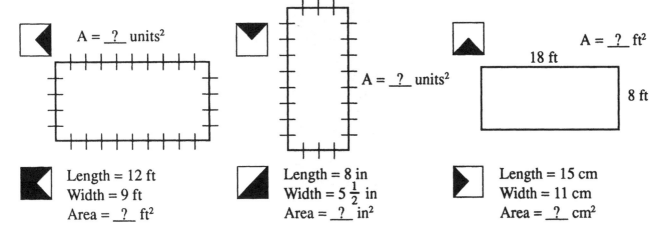

A = _?_ units²

A = _?_ units²

18 ft

8 ft

A = _?_ ft²

Length = 12 ft
Width = 9 ft
Area = _?_ ft²

Length = 8 in
Width = $5\frac{1}{2}$ in
Area = _?_ in²

Length = 15 cm
Width = 11 cm
Area = _?_ cm²

Find each missing measurement.

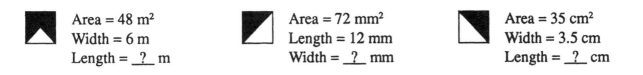

Area = 48 m²
Width = 6 m
Length = _?_ m

Area = 72 mm²
Length = 12 mm
Width = _?_ mm

Area = 35 cm²
Width = 3.5 cm
Length = _?_ cm

Find the area of each region.

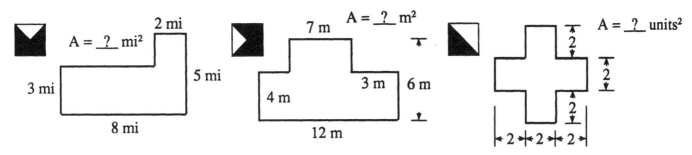

A = _?_ mi²

2 mi

3 mi

5 mi

8 mi

7 m

A = _?_ m²

4 m

3 m

6 m

12 m

A = _?_ units²

2

2

2

2 2 2

Measurement and Geometry by Design / Russell F. Jacobs   www.tessellations.com   © 1997 Jacobs Publishing Company

ACTIVITY 22

Name _____

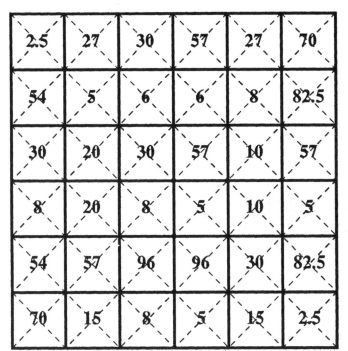

Here is the formula for the area of a triangle.

$$A = \frac{(Base)(Height)}{2}$$

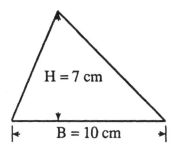

$H = 7$ cm

$B = 10$ cm

$$Area = \frac{(10)(7)}{2}$$
$$= 35 \text{ cm}^2$$

Find the area of each triangle.

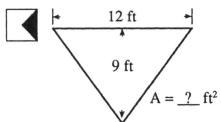

12 ft

9 ft

$A = \underline{\ ?\ }$ ft²

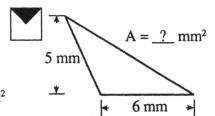

$A = \underline{\ ?\ }$ mm²

5 mm

6 mm

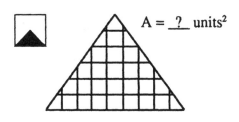

$A = \underline{\ ?\ }$ units²

Base = 5 yd
Height = 8 yd
Area = $\underline{\ ?\ }$ yd²

Base = 12 m
Height = 5 m
Area = $\underline{\ ?\ }$ m²

Base = 15 cm
Height = 11 cm
Area = $\underline{\ ?\ }$ cm²

Find each missing measurement.

Area = 12 ft²
Base = 4 ft
Height = $\underline{\ ?\ }$ ft

Area = 25 mi²
Base = $\underline{\ ?\ }$ mi
Height = 10 mi

Area = 50 cm²
Base = 12.5 cm
Height = $\underline{\ ?\ }$ cm

Find the area of each region.

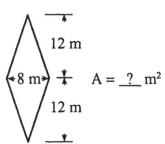

12 m

←8 m→

12 m

$A = \underline{\ ?\ }$ m²

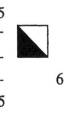
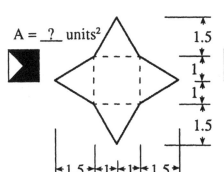

$A = \underline{\ ?\ }$ units²

1.5

1

1

1.5

←1.5→←1→←1→←1.5→

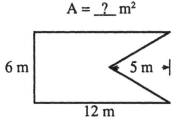

$A = \underline{\ ?\ }$ m²

6 m

5 m

12 m

ACTIVITY 23

30	115	45	40	75	50
130	40	95	50	45	35
50	30	25	110	50	95
40	45	25	110	40	45
130	50	45	40	95	35
45	105	30	50	105	40

A protractor is used to measure angles.

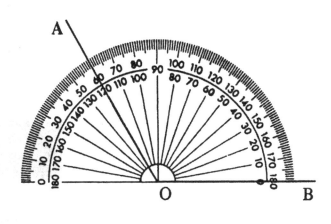

m ∠ AOB = 120°

Use a protractor to measure each angle to the nearest 5 degrees.

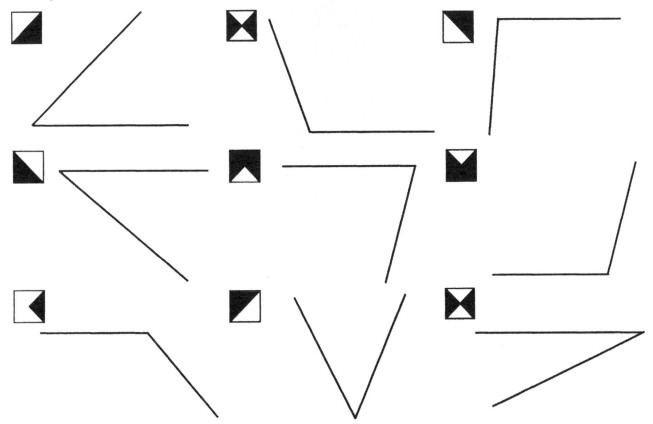

Measure each angle of triangle ABC to the nearest 5 degrees.

 m ∠ A = _?_ degrees   m ∠ B = _?_ degrees

 m ∠ C = _?_ degrees

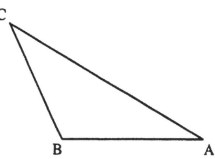

ACTIVITY 24

Name _____

140°	18	140°	120°	108°	120°
150°	120°	60°	24	140°	135°
36	108°	144°	162°	18	156°
120°	108°	120°	140°	18	140°
24	140°	135°	150°	120°	60°
162°	18	156°	36	108°	144°

The measure M in degrees of each angle of a regular polygon is given by this formula.

$$M = \frac{(n-2)180}{n}, \text{ n is}$$

the number of sides.

$$M = \frac{(4-2)180}{4}$$

n = 4

Square

$$M = \frac{(2)180}{4}$$

$$M = 90°$$

Find the measure of each angle of each regular polygon.

 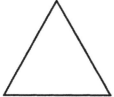   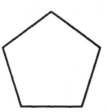   

 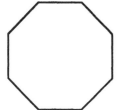   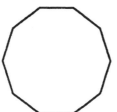   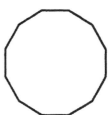

 9-sided polygon   15-sided polygon   20-sided polygon

Find the number of sides of each regular polygon.

 Measure of each angle is 160°   Measure of each angle is 165°   Measure of each angle is 170°

Measurement and Geometry by Design / Russell F. Jacobs   www.tessellations.com

Name _____

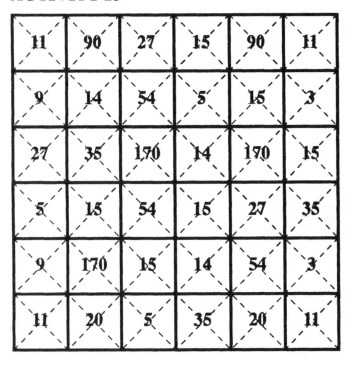

The number of diagonals D of any polygon is given by this formula.

$$D = \frac{n(n-3)}{2},$$

if n is the number of sides.

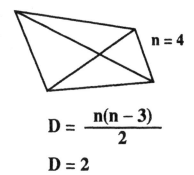

$$D = \frac{n(n-3)}{2}$$

$$D = 2$$

Find the number of diagonals of each regular polygon.

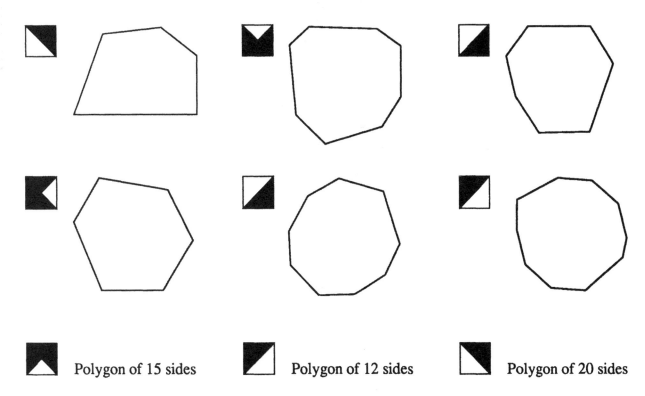

Polygon of 15 sides   Polygon of 12 sides   Polygon of 20 sides

Find the number of sides of each polygon.

 Polygon with 44 diagonals

 Polygon with 0 diagonals

 Polygon with 90 diagonals

ACTIVITY 26

Name _____

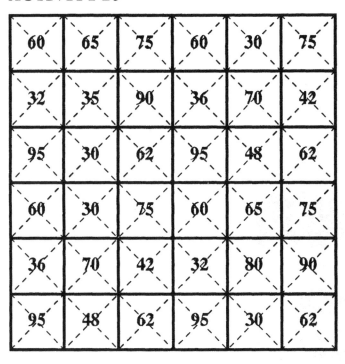

60	65	75	60	30	75
32	35	90	36	70	42
95	30	62	95	48	62
60	30	75	60	65	75
36	70	42	32	80	90
95	48	62	95	30	62

The sum of the measures of the angles of a triangle is 180°.

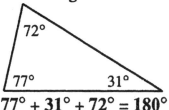

$$77° + 31° + 72° = 180°$$

The measure of an exterior angle of a triangle equals the sum of the measures of the two opposite interior angles.

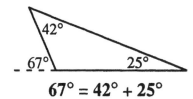

$$67° = 42° + 25°$$

Find the value of n *for each triangle.*

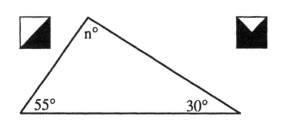

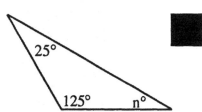

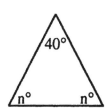

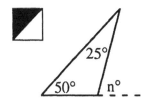

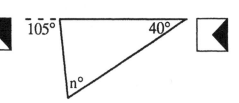

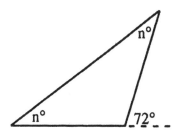

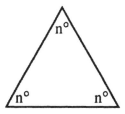

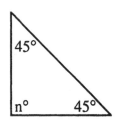

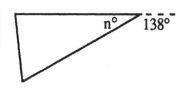

 $n° + n° + 56° = 180°$

 $180° - n° = 148°$

 $102° = 54° + n°$

ACTIVITY 27

Name _____

50°	200°	45°	55°	180°	50°
45°	24°	110°	220°	24°	55°
200°	90°	100°	200°	90°	180°
55°	160°	45°	55°	160°	45°
100°	24°	110°	40°	24°	200°
50°	55°	180°	200°	45°	50°

The measure of an inscribed angle of a circle equals one-half the measure of its intercepted arc.

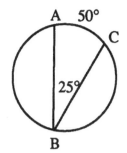

m angle ABC = $\frac{1}{2}$ m arc AC

= $\frac{1}{2} \times 50$

= 25°

Find the measure of each angle ABC.

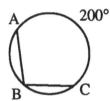

m arc AC = 200°

m arc AC = 48°

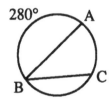

m arc ABC = 280°

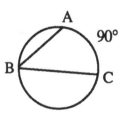

m arc AC = 90°

m arc AC = 180°

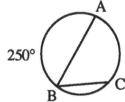

m arc ABC = 250°

Find the measure of each arc AC.

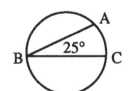

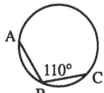
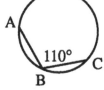

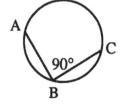

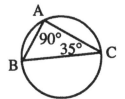
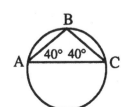

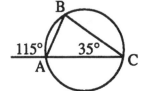

ACTIVITY 28

Name _____

The volume of a rectangular solid is the number of cubic units it contains. This solid has a volume of 24 cubic units.

72	80	150	27	64	72
36	76	54	54	96	10
64	21	10	36	16	80
96	16	27	150	21	76
150	80	54	54	64	27
72	76	36	10	96	72

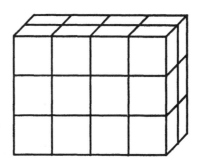

Volume = length × width × height
$$V = 4 \times 2 \times 3$$
$$V = 24 \text{ units}^3 \text{ (cubic units)}$$

Find the volume of each solid in cubic units (units³).

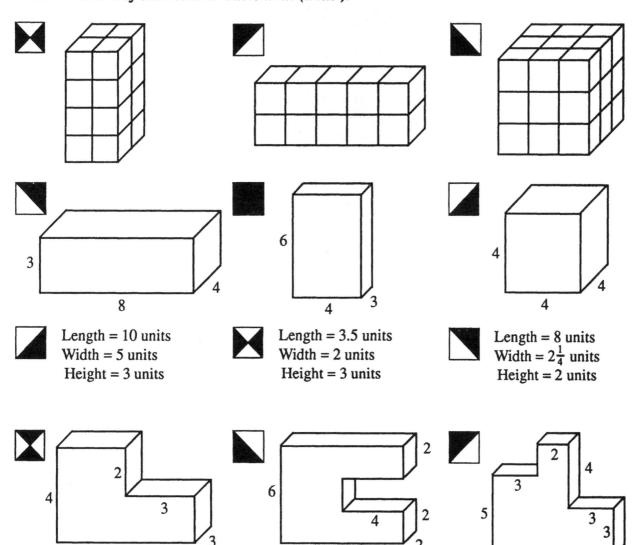

Length = 10 units
Width = 5 units
Height = 3 units

Length = 3.5 units
Width = 2 units
Height = 3 units

Length = 8 units
Width = $2\frac{1}{4}$ units
Height = 2 units

ACTIVITY 29

Name _____

75°	58°	31°	90°	58°	140°
55°	130°	75°	140°	150°	55°
150°	60°	130°	122°	80°	130°
90°	70°	31°	90°	70°	31°
58°	31°	75°	140°	90°	58°
75°	55°	130°	122°	55°	140°

In this circle, the measure of angle AOD equals one-half the sum of the measures of arc AD and arc BC.

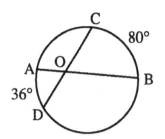

$$m \text{ angle } AOD = \frac{m \text{ arc } AD + m \text{ arc } BC}{2}$$

$$= \frac{36° + 80°}{2}$$

$$= 58°$$

Find the measure of each angle AOD.

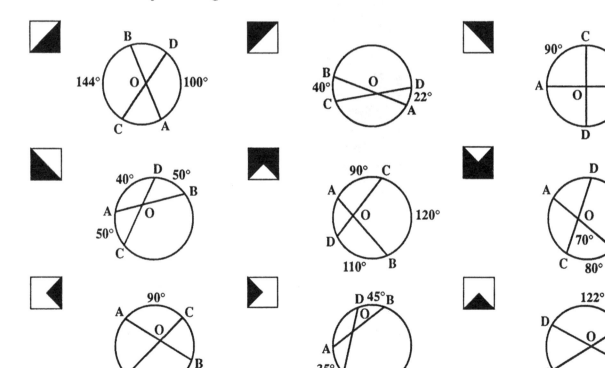

Find the measure of each arc AC.

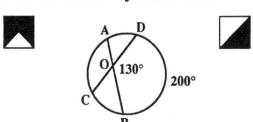

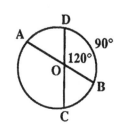

ACTIVITY 30

Name _____

20°	12°	70°	30°	110°	38°
110°	62°	110°	90°	120°	60°
38°	50°	30°	70°	110°	106°
30°	110°	38°	20°	12°	70°
90°	65°	60°	110°	55°	110°
70°	110°	106°	38°	50°	30°

In this circle, the measure of angle AOC equals one-half the difference of the measures of arc AC and arc BD.

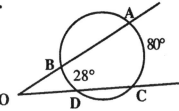

m angle AOC

$$= \frac{1}{2}(\text{m arc AC} - \text{m arc BD})$$

$$= \frac{1}{2}(80 - 28)$$

$$= \frac{1}{2}(52)$$

$$= 26°$$

Find the measure of each angle AOC.

Find the measure of each arc AC.

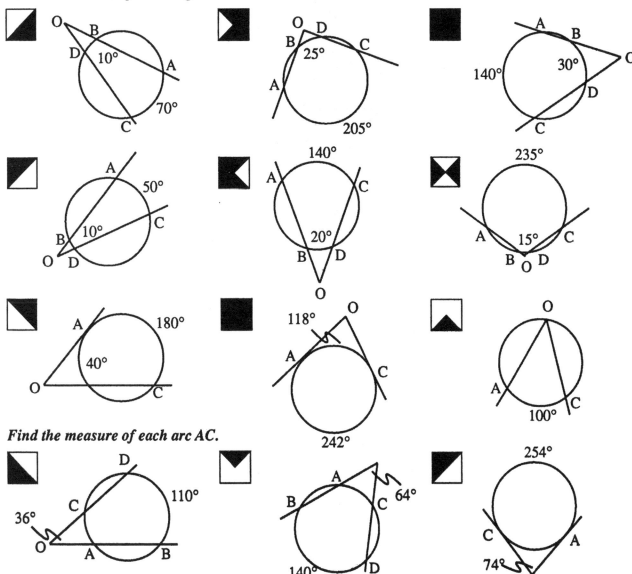

ACTIVITY 31

Name _____

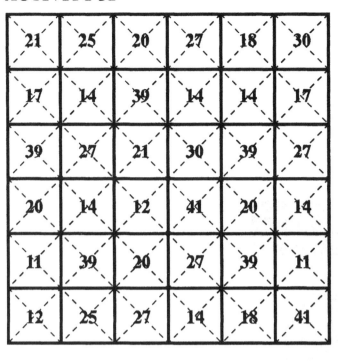

Estimate the number of square units in each area. Count each square if half or more of it is contained in the figure. Do not count a square if less than half of it is in the figure.

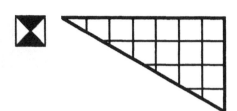

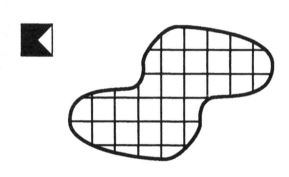

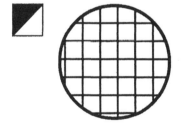

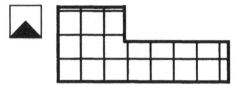

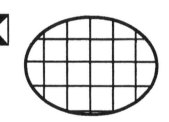

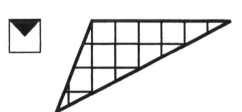

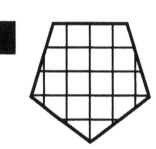

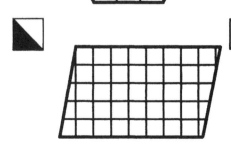

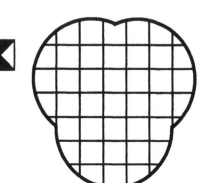

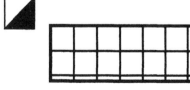

ACTIVITY 32

10.5	4.5	109.9	75.36	4.5	9.42
12.56	7.85	10.5	25.12	7.85	6.28
109.9	10.5	18.84	5	9.42	75.36
9.42	75.36	5	18.84	109.9	10.5
12.56	7.85	75.36	109.9	7.85	6.28
75.36	4.71	25.12	10.5	4.71	109.9

The circumference of a circle can be found as follows.

Circumference = π × diameter

C = πd

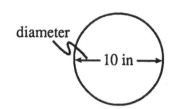

Let π = 3.14 and d = 10 in.

$$C = (3.14)(10)$$
$$C = 31.4 \text{ in}$$

Find the circumference of each circle. Let π = 3.14.

C = _?_ ft

 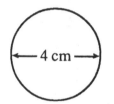
C = _?_ cm

 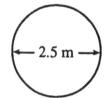
C = _?_ m

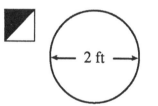
C = _?_ in

 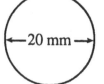
C = _?_ cm

 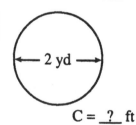
C = _?_ ft

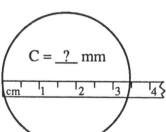
C = _?_ mm

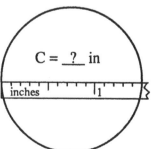
C = _?_ in

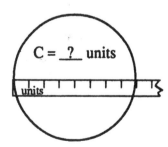
C = _?_ units

Find the diameter of each circle. d = C ÷ π. Let π = 3.14.

 C = 15.7 cm

d = _?_ cm

 C = 14.13 ft

d = _?_ ft

 C = 32.97 mm

d = _?_ mm

Measurement and Geometry by Design / Russell F. Jacobs   www.tessellations.com   © 1997 Jacobs Publishing Company

Name _____

15	22	1.1304	0.785	12.56	78.5
0.1256	18	0.0314	0.0314	23	7.065
3.14	7.065	78.5	15	0.1256	16
0.785	7.065	15	78.5	0.1256	1.1304
0.1256	20	22	12.56	13	7.065
15	0.0314	50.24	3.14	0.0314	78.5

The area of a circle can be found as follows.

$$A = \pi r^2$$

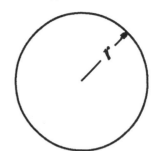

Let π = 3.14 and r = 3 cm
$$A = (3.14)(3^2)$$
$$A = (3.14)(9)$$
$$A = 28.26 \text{ cm}^2$$

Find the area of each circle. Let π = 3.14.

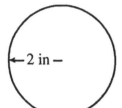

← 2 in →

A = _?_ in²

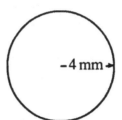

– 4 mm –

A = _?_ mm²

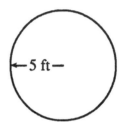

← 5 ft →

A = _?_ ft²

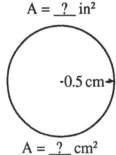

–0.5 cm→

A = _?_ cm²

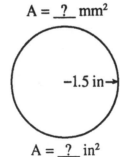

–1.5 in→

A = _?_ in²

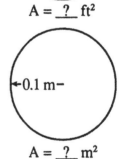

←0.1 m–

A = _?_ m²

Find each area. $A = \frac{\pi d^2}{4}$, if d is the diameter. Let π = 3.14.

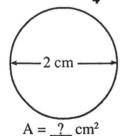

←— 2 cm —→

A = _?_ cm²

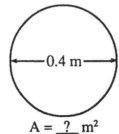

←—0.4 m—→

A = _?_ m²

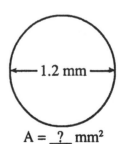

←— 1.2 mm —→

A = _?_ mm²

Which circle has the greatest area?

12. Diameter = 4 in
13. Radius = 2 in
14. Circumference = 15 in
15. Diameter = 0.5 ft

16. Radius = 15 mm
17. Diameter = 1.4 cm
18. Circumference = 4 cm
19. Diameter = 0.01 m

20. Circumference = 30 mm
21. Circumference = 0.03 m
22. Diameter = 1.7 cm
23. Diameter = 16 mm

ACTIVITY 34

Name _____

35	10	20	21	26	7
30	15	24	24	8	30
7	26	25	20	10	13
25	26	7	35	10	20
24	8	30	30	15	24
20	10	13	7	26	21

Right Triangle Rule

In a right triangle, the square of the length of the hypotenuse (longest side) equals the sum of the squares of the lengths of the legs (shorter sides).

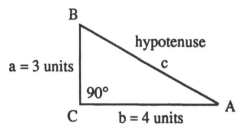

In triangle ABC, $c^2 = a^2 + b^2$

$$c^2 = 3^2 + 4^2$$
$$c^2 = 9 + 16$$
$$c^2 = 25$$
$$c = \sqrt{25}$$
$$c = 5$$

Find the length of each hypotenuse. Refer to the Table of Squares, if needed.

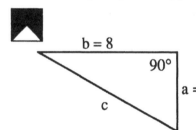

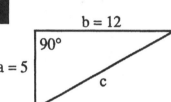

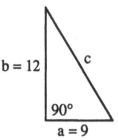

  a = 12 units
b = 16 units
c = _?_ units

  a = 10 units
b = 24 units
c = _?_ units

  a = 15 units
b = 20 units
c = _?_ units

Find the missing length of a leg. Formulas: $a = \sqrt{c^2 - b^2}$ $b = \sqrt{c^2 - a^2}$

  b = 24 units
c = 25 units
a = _?_ units

  a = 15 units
c = 17 units
b = _?_ units

  b = 16 units
c = 34 units
a = _?_ units

Find the missing length if each triangle is a right triangle.

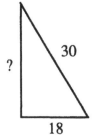

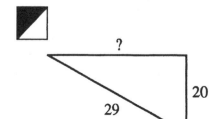

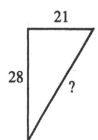

ACTIVITY 35

Name _____

10	1.7	7.5	7	10	5.1
6	6.8	10.2	5	6	6.8
13.6	8	10	1.7	8	13.6
8.5	8	6	6.8	8	8.5
10	5.1	10.2	5	10	5.1
6	6.8	7.5	7	6	6.8

This is a 30° − 60° right triangle.

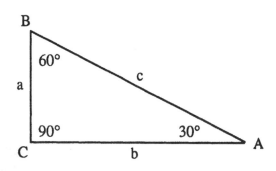

Formulas:

$$a = \tfrac{1}{2}c$$
$$b = \tfrac{1}{2}c\sqrt{3}$$

Find a in each right triangle.

 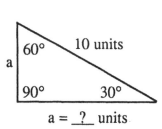

a = _?_ units

 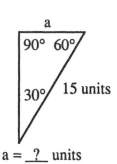

a = _?_ units

 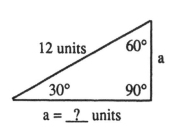

a = _?_ units

Find b in each right triangle. Use 1.7 as an approximation for $\sqrt{3}$.

 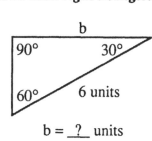

b = _?_ units

 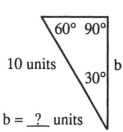

b = _?_ units

 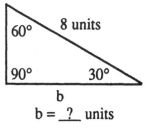

b = _?_ units

Find c in each 30° − 60° right triangle if a is the length of the leg opposite the 30° angle.

 a = 4 units
c = _?_ units

 a = 3.5 units
c = _?_ units

 a = 5 units
c = _?_ units

Find b in each 30° − 60° right triangle if b is the length of the leg opposite the 60° angle and c is the length of the hypotenuse. Let $\sqrt{3}$ = 1.7.

 c = 12 units
b = _?_ units

c = 2 units
b = _?_ units

 c = 16 units
b = _?_ units

ACTIVITY 36

Name _____

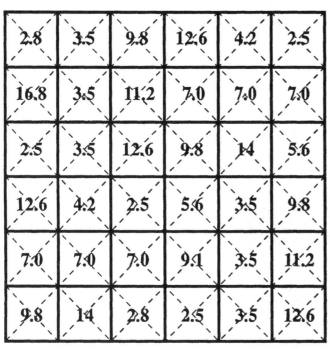

This is a 45° − 45° right triangle.

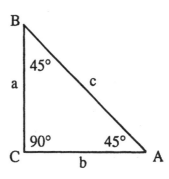

Formulas:
$$a = \tfrac{1}{2}c\sqrt{2}\,;\; c = a\sqrt{2}$$
$$b = \tfrac{1}{2}c\sqrt{2}\,;\; c = b\sqrt{2}$$

Find a in each right triangle. Use 1.4 as an approximation for $\sqrt{2}$.

 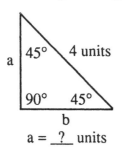

a = __?__ units

 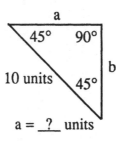

a = __?__ units

 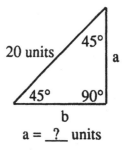

a = __?__ units

Find b in each 45° − 45° right triangle if a is the length of a leg and c is the length of the hypotenuse. Let $\sqrt{2}$ = 1.4.

    a = 2.5 units
b = __?__ units

c = 16 units
b = __?__ units

c = 13 units
b = __?__ units

Find c in each right triangle. Let $\sqrt{2}$ = 1.4.

 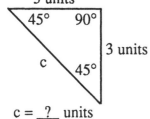

c = __?__ units

c = __?__ units

 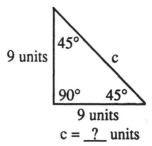

c = __?__ units

c = __?__ units

Find each unknown length. Let $\sqrt{2}$ = 1.4.

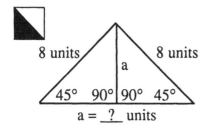

a = __?__ units

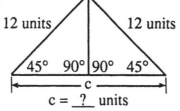

c = __?__ units

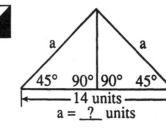

a = __?__ units

Name _____

0.75	60	50	0.4	1.732	0.75
0.268	75	65	65	0.268	75
1.000	35	25	25	1.000	35
1.000	35	25	25	1.000	35
1.732	0.5	50	0.4	1.732	60
0.75	75	65	65	0.268	0.75

The **tangent** of an acute angle of a right triangle equals the length of the opposite leg divided by the length of the adjacent leg.

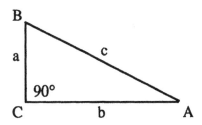

Formulas:

$$\tan \angle A = \frac{a}{b}$$

$$\tan \angle B = \frac{b}{a}$$

Find tan ∠A in each right triangle. Express as a decimal.

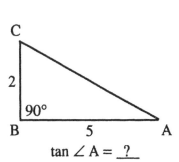

tan ∠ A = _?_

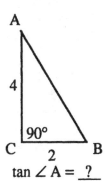

tan ∠ A = _?_

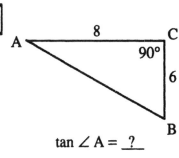

tan ∠ A = _?_

Use the Table of Sines, Cosines, and Tangents to find each value.

 tan 15° = _?_

 tan 45° = _?_

 tan 60° = _?_

Use the Table of Sines, Cosines, and Tangents to find the measure of ∠A to the nearest 5°.

tan ∠ A = 0.5
m ∠ A = _?_ degrees

tan ∠ A = 3.6
m ∠ A = _?_ degrees

tan ∠ A = 1.2
m ∠ A = _?_ degrees

Use the meaning of tangent and the Table of Sines, Cosines, and Tangents to find each required measure.

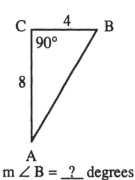

m ∠ B = _?_ degrees

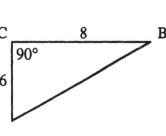
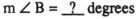

m ∠ B = _?_ degrees

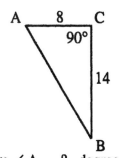

m ∠ A = _?_ degrees

Name _____

0.996	55	75	75	0.55	30
15	0.500	15	15	0.996	15
0.766	55	0.75	45	0.55	0.6
0.766	55	0.500	0.996	55	0.6
15	0.75	15	15	45	15
45	0.55	50	50	0.55	0.75

The <u>sine</u> of an acute angle of a right triangle equals the length of the opposite leg divided by the length of the hypotenuse.

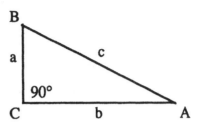

Formulas:

$$\sin \angle A = \frac{a}{c}$$

$$\sin \angle B = \frac{b}{c}$$

Find sin ∠A in each right triangle. Express as a decimal.

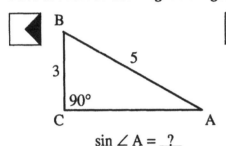

$\sin \angle A = $ __?__

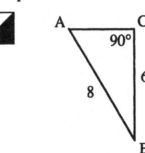

$\sin \angle A = $ __?__

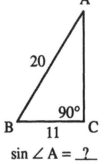

$\sin \angle A = $ __?__

Use the Table of Sines, Cosines, and Tangents to find each value.

 $\sin 30° = $ __?__

 $\sin 50° = $ __?__

 $\sin 85° = $ __?__

Use the Table of Sines, Cosines, and Tangents to find the measure of ∠A to the nearest 5°.

 $\sin \angle A = 0.243$
$m \angle A = $ __?__ degrees

 $\sin \angle A = 0.715$
$m \angle A = $ __?__ degrees

 $\sin \angle A = 0.955$
$m \angle A = $ __?__ degrees

Use the meaning of sine and the Table of Sines, Cosines, and Tangents to find each required measure.

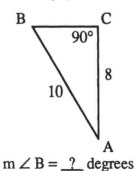

$m \angle B = $ __?__ degrees

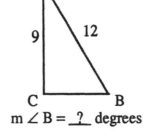

$m \angle B = $ __?__ degrees

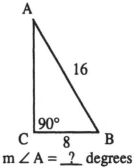

$m \angle A = $ __?__ degrees

ACTIVITY 39

Name _____

30	70	0.707	0.707	70	0.9
80	0.9	45	0.342	30	50
50	0.7	0.9	30	25	80
50	0.342	0.9	0.9	0.966	80
80	30	25	0.7	30	50
0.9	0.5	70	70	0.5	30

The <u>cosine</u> of an acute angle of a right triangle equals the length of the adjacent leg divided by the length of the hypotenuse.

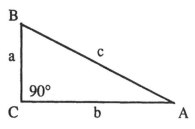

Formulas:

$$\cos \angle A = \frac{b}{c}$$

$$\cos \angle B = \frac{a}{c}$$

Find cos ∠A in each right triangle. Express as a decimal.

 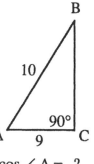

cos ∠ A = _?_

 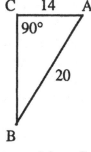

cos ∠ A = _?_

 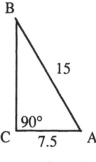

cos ∠ A = _?_

Use the Table of Sines, Cosines, and Tangents to find each value.

 cos 15° = _?_

 cos 45° = _?_

 cos 70° = _?_

Use the Table of Sines, Cosines, and Tangents to find the measure of ∠A to the nearest 5°.

 cos ∠ A = 0.175
m ∠ A = _?_ degrees

 cos ∠ A = 0.900
m ∠ A = _?_ degrees

 cos ∠ A = 0.655
m ∠ A = _?_ degrees

Use the meaning of <u>cosine</u> and the Table of Sines, Cosines, and Tangents to find each required measure.

 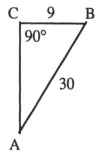

m ∠ B = _?_ degrees

 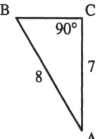

m ∠ A = _?_ degrees

 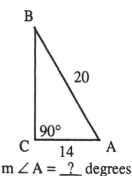

m ∠ A = _?_ degrees

Measurement and Geometry by Design / Russell F. Jacobs   www.tessellations.com   © 1997 Jacobs Publishing Company

ACTIVITY 40

8.568	8.241	2.115	1.692	45	8.568
2,115	75	5,656	6.43	75	1.692
4.242	5.77	45	8.241	5.77	45
1,692	5.77	2,115	1.692	5.77	2,115
45	20	6.43	5,656	12.86	4,242
8,568	1.692	45	8,241	2.115	8,568

The Table of Sines, Cosines, and Tangents can used to find lengths of sides of right triangles.

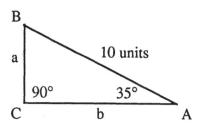

$$\sin 35° = \frac{a}{10} \qquad \cos 35° = \frac{b}{10}$$
$$a = (10)(\sin 35°) \qquad b = (10)(\cos 35°)$$
$$a = (10)(0.574) \qquad b = (10)(0.819)$$
$$a = 5.74 \qquad b = 8.19$$

Find a in each right triangle.

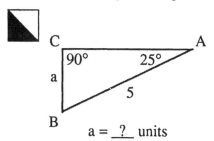

a = __?__ units

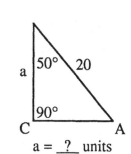

a = __?__ units

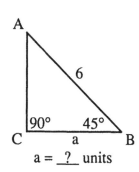

a = __?__ units

Find b in each right triangle.

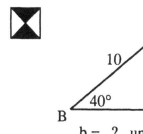

b = __?__ units

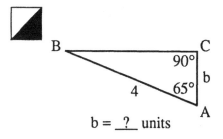

b = __?__ units

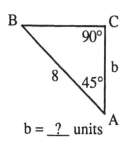

b = __?__ units

Use tan ∠A to find a in each right triangle.

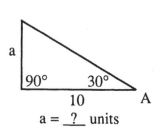

a = __?__ units

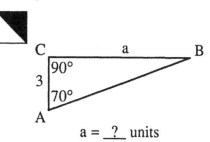

a = __?__ units

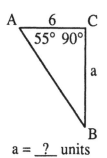

a = __?__ units

Refer to the Table of Sines, Cosines, and Tangents.

 sin 15° = cos __?__ °

 cos 70° = sin __?__ °

 sin 45° = cos __?__ °

Measurement and Geometry by Design / Russell F. Jacobs   www.tessellations.com

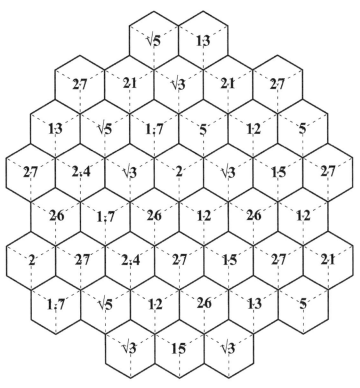

From the Pythagorean theorem, the diagonal d of the rectangle ab is given by $d = (a^2 + b^2)^{1/2}$, from which $d^2 = a^2 + b^2$.

Similarly, the space diagonal e of the cuboid is the diagonal of the rectangle cd:
$$e = (d^2 + c^2)^{1/2}$$
$$= (a^2 + b^2 + c^2)^{1/2}.$$

You will need a calculator for this activity.

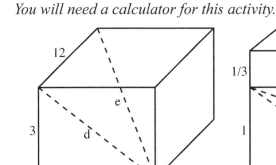

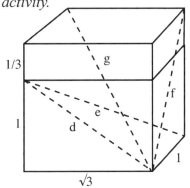

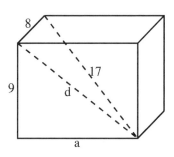

 For the cuboid shown above, what is the value of d?

 For the lower cuboid shown above, what is the value of d?

 For the cuboid shown above, what is the value of d?

 What is the value of e?

 What is the value of e?

 What is the value of a?

 What is the space diagonal of a unit cube (one in which each edge has length 1)?

 For the two cuboids together, what is the approximate value of f (to one digit after the decimal)?

 If the cuboid above were doubled in length (left to right dimension), what would be the value of d, to the nearest whole number?

 If each edge were 12 inches, what would the space diagonal be in inches, to the nearest whole number?

 What is the approximate value of g?

 What would be the length of the space diagonal to the nearest whole number?

ACTIVITY 42

Name _____

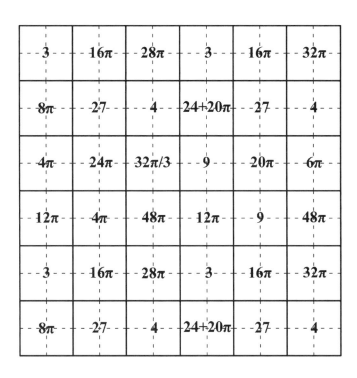

3	16π	28π	3	16π	32π
8π	27	4	24+20π	27	4
4π	24π	32π/3	9	20π	6π
12π	4π	48π	12π	9	48π
3	16π	28π	3	16π	32π
8π	27	4	24+20π	27	4

Answer the following questions about spheres, cones, and cylinders.

Sphere
$C = 2\pi r$
$A_S = 4\pi r^2$
$V = 4\pi r^3/3$

Cylinder
$C = 2\pi r$
$A_S = 2\pi r^2 + 2\pi rh$
$V = \pi r^2 h$

Cone
$C = 2\pi r$
$A_S = \pi r^2 + \pi r(r^2 + h^2)^{1/2}$
$V = \pi r^2 h/3$

 What is the circumference of a sphere of radius 2?

 What is its surface area?

 What is its volume?

 What is the surface area of a cone with radius of 3 and height of 4?

 What is its volume?

Consider a sphere of radius 3 and a cone of radius 3 and height 3. How many times larger is the volume of the sphere compared to the volume of the cone?

 What is the circumference of a cylinder of radius 4?

 What is its surface area if its height is 2?

 What is its volume?

 If all of it's dimensions are tripled, how many times larger is its circumference?

 How many times larger is its area?

 How many times larger is its volume?

 If a sphere of radius 1 is cut in half, what is the total surface area of the two hemispheres?

 What is the surface area of a cylinder of radius 2 and height 3?

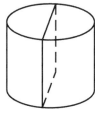

 If the cylinder (of radius 2 and height 3) is cut in half vertically as shown, what is the total surface area of the two halves?

 If it's cut in half horizontally (parallel to the base), what is the total area of the two halves?

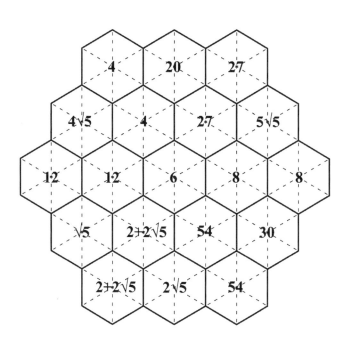

Tetrahedron

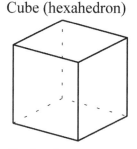
Cube (hexahedron)

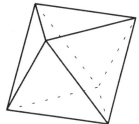
Octahedron

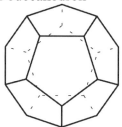
Dodecahedron

Icosahedron

A polyhedron is a three-dimensional solid, the faces of which are polygons. The Platonic Solids are the five regular polyhedra, with faces that are all the same type of regular polygon and all arranged in the same manner. A point at which three or more polygons meet is a vertex, and a line along which two polygons meet is an edge.

How many faces does a dodecahedron have?

How many faces does an icosahedron have?

How many vertices does a tetrahedron have?

How many vertices does an hexahedron have?

How many edges does a tetrahedron have?

How many edges does a dodecahedron have?

An equilateral triangle with edge length 1 has an area of $\sqrt{5}/4$.

What is the surface area of a tetrahedron with edges of length 1?

What is the surface area of an octahedron with edges of length 1?

What is the surface area of an icosahedron with edges of length 1?

What is the surface area of a tetrahedron with edges of length 2?

What is the surface area of a cube with edge length 3?

What is its volume?

If an octahedron with edge length 1 were split in half as shown, what would its total surface area be?

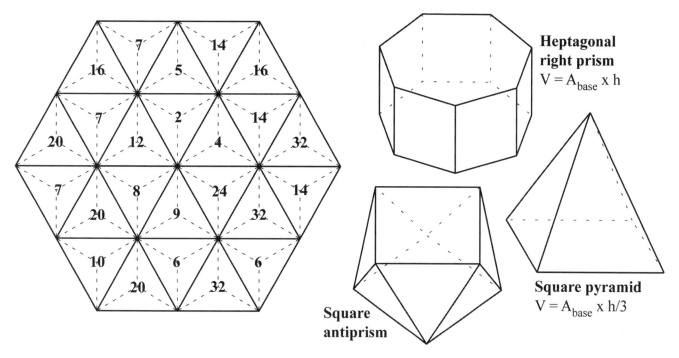

Heptagonal right prism
$V = A_{base} \times h$

Square antiprism

Square pyramid
$V = A_{base} \times h/3$

A prism is a polyhedron with two faces that are congruent polygons and sides that are parallelograms. An anti-prism is a polyhedron with two faces that are congruent polygons and sides that are isosceles triangles. A (regular) pyramid is a polyhedron with a regular polygon as its base and all other faces triangles meeting at a common vertex, known as the apex. The volume formulas above are true for all right prisms and all pyramids.

 If a hexagonal prism has base area of 4 and height of 4, what is its volume?

 How many faces does a pentagonal prism have?

 How many edges does a pentagonal antiprism have?

 What is the volume of a square prism with a base measuring 2 x 2 and a height of three?

 How many faces does a hexagonal prism have?

 How many edges does a hexagonal antiprism have?

 What is the surface area of the same square prism?

 How many faces does an octagonal prism have?

 How many faces does a hexagonal antiprism have?

 What is the volume of a square pyramid with the same base and height?

 Fill in the blank to complete the formula for the number of faces possessed by a prism for which the top and bottom faces are n-sided regular polygons.

$F = n +$ ____

 If the pyramid's base were 3 x 3 instead 2 x 2, what would its volume be?

How many faces does a square pyramid have?

How many vertices does an pentagonal pyramid have?

Table of Sines, Cosines and Tangents

Measure of angle	Sine	Cosine	Tangent
5°	0.087	0.996	0.087
10°	0.174	0.985	0.176
15°	0.259	0.966	0.268
20°	0.342	0.940	0.364
25°	0.423	0.906	0.466
30°	0.500	0.866	0.577
35°	0.574	0.819	0.700
40°	0.643	0.766	0.839
45°	0.707	0.707	1.000
50°	0.766	0.643	1.192
55°	0.819	0.574	1.428
60°	0.866	0.500	1.732
65°	0.906	0.423	2.145
70°	0.940	0.342	2.747
75°	0.966	0.259	3.732
80°	0.985	0.174	5.671
85°	0.996	0.087	11.430

Table of Squares

Number	Square	Number	Square	Number	Square
1	1	13	169	25	625
2	4	14	196	26	676
3	9	15	225	27	729
4	16	16	256	28	784
5	25	17	289	29	841
6	36	18	324	30	900
7	49	19	361	31	961
8	64	20	400	32	1024
9	81	21	441	33	1089
10	100	22	484	34	1156
11	121	23	529	35	1225
12	144	24	576	36	1296

Metric Measures

Length
10 millimeters (mm) = 1 centimeter (cm)
10 centimeters (cm) = 1 decimeter (dm)
10 decimeters (dm) = 1 meter (m)
10 meters (m) = 1 dekameter (dam)
10 dekameters (dam) = 1 hectometer (hm)
10 hectometers (hm) = 1 kilometer (km)

Mass
10 milligrams (mg) = 1 centigram (cg)
10 centigrams (cg) = 1 decigram (dg)
10 decigrams (dg) = 1 gram (g)
10 grams (g) = 1 dekagram (dag)
10 dekagrams (dag) = 1 hectogram (hg)
10 hectograms (hg) = 1 kilogram (kg)

Capacity
10 milliliters (mℓ) = 1 centiliter (cℓ)
10 centiliters (cℓ) = 1 deciliter (dℓ)
10 deciliters (dℓ) = 1 liter (ℓ)
10 liters (ℓ) = 1 dekaliter (daℓ)
10 dekaliters (daℓ) = 1 hectoliter (hℓ)
10 hectoliters (hℓ) = 1 kiloliter (kℓ)

Special Measures
1 fathom = 6 feet
1 furlong = 660 feet
8 furlongs = 1 mile
1 league = 3 miles

Customary Measures

Length
12 inches (in) = 1 foot (ft)
3 feet (ft) = 1 yard (yd)
$16\frac{1}{2}$ feet (ft) = 1 rod (rd)
$5\frac{1}{2}$ yards (yd) = 1 rod (rd)
1,760 yards (yd) = 1 mile (mi)
5,280 feet (ft) = 1 mile (mi)

Mass
16 ounces (oz) = 1 pound (lb)
2,000 pounds (lb) = 1 ton (T)

Capacity
8 fluid ounces (fl oz) = 1 cup (c)
2 cups (c) = 1 pint (pt)
2 pints (pt) = 1 quart (qt)
4 quarts (qt) = 1 gallon (gal)

1 firkin = 9 gallons
1 hogshead = 63 gallons
4 pecks = 1 bushel
1 hand = 4 inches
1 bolt = 120 feet

Metric/Customary
Approximate Equivalents

Metric	Customary	Customary	Metric
1 cm	0.4 in	1 in	2.5 cm
1 m	39.37 in	1 in	0.025 m
1 m	1.09 yd	1 yd	0.9 m
1 km	0.62 mi	1 mi	1.6 km
1 g	0.035 oz	1 oz	28.3 g
1 kg	2.2 lb	1 lb	0.45 kg
1 ℓ	1.06 qt	1 qt	0.95 ℓ
1 ℓ	0.26 gal	1 gal	3.8 ℓ

Answer Key

ACTIVITY 1

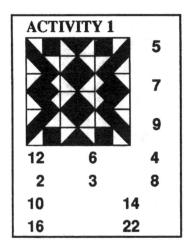

5

7

9

12	6	4
2	3	8
10		14
16		22

ACTIVITY 2

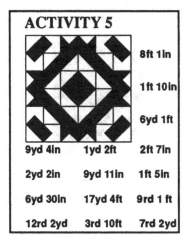

$\frac{15}{8}$

$\frac{9}{4}$

$\frac{5}{2}$

1	$\frac{8}{6}$	$\frac{15}{12}$
$\frac{12}{10}$	$\frac{7}{5}$	$\frac{4}{3}$
$\frac{5}{4}$	3	$\frac{10}{2}$
$\frac{43}{8}$	$\frac{22}{8}$	$\frac{19}{4}$

ACTIVITY 3

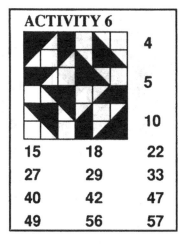

3

2.5

4

2.4	24	3.5
4.5	7	89
105	13	47
7.5	9	10.5

ACTIVITY 4

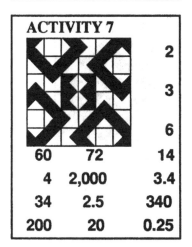

7

3

10		5
4		2
20	12	6
9	13	21
$2\frac{1}{2}$	$2\frac{3}{4}$	$4\frac{1}{2}$

ACTIVITY 5

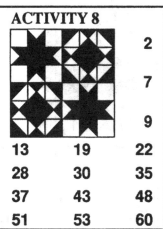

8ft 1in

1ft 10in

6yd 1ft

9yd 4in	1yd 2ft	2ft 7in
2yd 2in	9yd 11in	1ft 5in
6yd 30in	17yd 4ft	9rd 1 ft
12rd 2yd	3rd 10ft	7rd 2yd

ACTIVITY 6

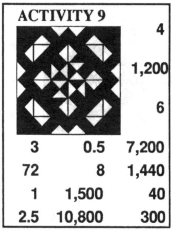

4

5

10

15	18	22
27	29	33
40	42	47
49	56	57

ACTIVITY 7

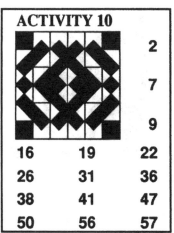

2

3

6

60	72	14
4	2,000	3.4
34	2.5	340
200	20	0.25

ACTIVITY 8

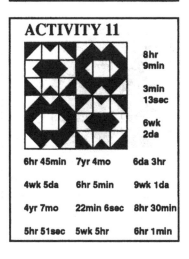

2

7

9

13	19	22
28	30	35
37	43	48
51	53	60

ACTIVITY 9

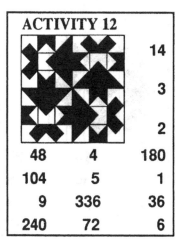

4

1,200

6

3	0.5	7,200
72	8	1,440
1	1,500	40
2.5	10,800	300

ACTIVITY 10

2

7

9

16	19	22
26	31	36
38	41	47
50	56	57

ACTIVITY 11

8hr 9min

3min 13sec

6wk 2da

6hr 45min	7yr 4mo	6da 3hr
4wk 5da	6hr 5min	9wk 1da
4yr 7mo	22min 6sec	8hr 30min
5hr 51sec	5wk 5hr	6hr 1min

ACTIVITY 12

14

3

2

48	4	180
104	5	1
9	336	36
240	72	6

ACTIVITY 13

6:00
3:00
5:00   4:00   2:00
3:30   10:00   8:00
1:30   2:30   8:30
7:00   12:30
11:00   9:00

ACTIVITY 14

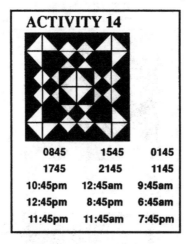

0845   1545   0145
1745   2145   1145
10:45pm   12:45am   9:45am
12:45pm   8:45pm   6:45am
11:45pm   11:45am   7:45pm

ACTIVITY 15

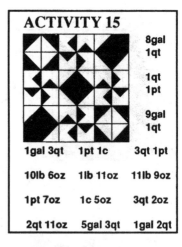

8gal
1qt

1qt
1pt

9gal
1qt

1gal 3qt   1pt 1c   3qt 1pt
10lb 6oz   1lb 11oz   11lb 9oz
1pt 7oz   1c 5oz   3qt 2oz
2qt 11oz   5gal 3qt   1gal 2qt

ACTIVITY 16

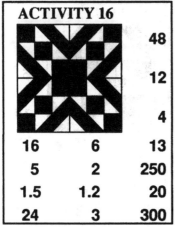

48
12
4
16   6   13
5   2   250
1.5   1.2   20
24   3   300

ACTIVITY 17

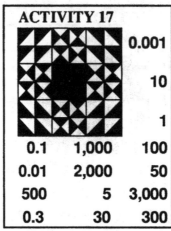

0.001
10
1
0.1   1,000   100
0.01   2,000   50
500   5   3,000
0.3   30   300

ACTIVITY 18

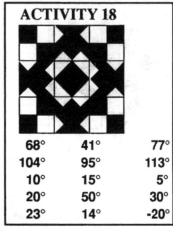

68°   41°   77°
104°   95°   113°
10°   15°   5°
20°   50°   30°
23°   14°   -20°

ACTIVITY 19

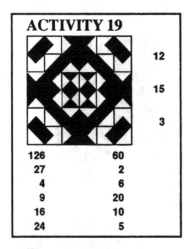

12
15
3
126   60
27   2
4   6
9   20
16   10
24   5

ACTIVITY 20

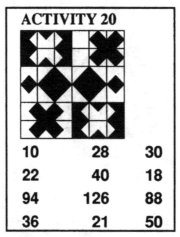

10   28   30
22   40   18
94   126   88
36   21   50

ACTIVITY 21

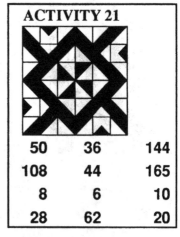

50   36   144
108   44   165
8   6   10
28   62   20

ACTIVITY 22

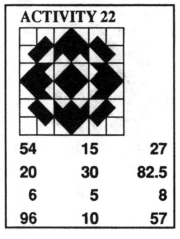

54   15   27
20   30   82.5
6   5   8
96   10   57

ACTIVITY 23

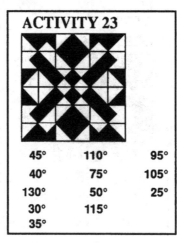

45°   110°   95°
40°   75°   105°
130°   50°   25°
30°   115°
35°

ACTIVITY 24

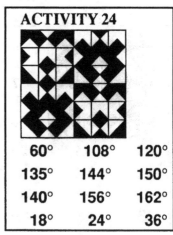

60°   108°   120°
135°   144°   150°
140°   156°   162°
18°   24°   36°

ACTIVITY 25

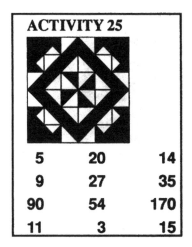

5	20	14
9	27	35
90	54	170
11	3	15

ACTIVITY 26

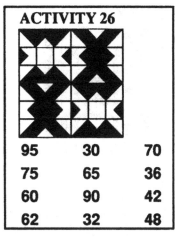

95	30	70
75	65	36
60	90	42
62	32	48

ACTIVITY 27

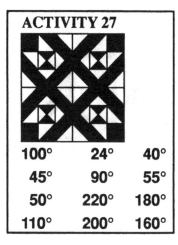

100°	24°	40°
45°	90°	55°
50°	220°	180°
110°	200°	160°

ACTIVITY 28

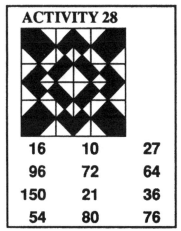

16	10	27
96	72	64
150	21	36
54	80	76

ACTIVITY 29

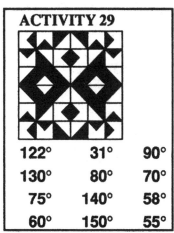

122°	31°	90°
130°	80°	70°
75°	140°	58°
60°	150°	55°

ACTIVITY 30

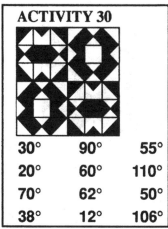

30°	90°	55°
20°	60°	110°
70°	62°	50°
38°	12°	106°

ACTIVITY 31

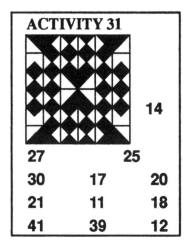

		14
27		25
30	17	20
21	11	18
41	39	12

ACTIVITY 32

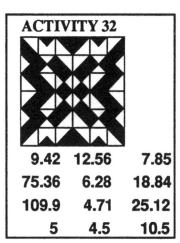

9.42	12.56	7.85
75.36	6.28	18.84
109.9	4.71	25.12
5	4.5	10.5

ACTIVITY 33

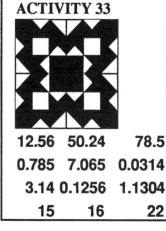

12.56	50.24	78.5
0.785	7.065	0.0314
3.14	0.1256	1.1304
15	16	22

ACTIVITY 34

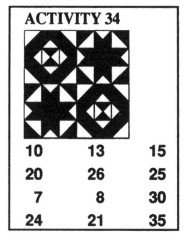

10	13	15
20	26	25
7	8	30
24	21	35

ACTIVITY 35

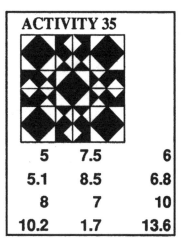

5	7.5	6
5.1	8.5	6.8
8	7	10
10.2	1.7	13.6

ACTIVITY 36

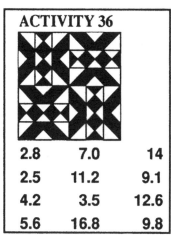

2.8	7.0	14
2.5	11.2	9.1
4.2	3.5	12.6
5.6	16.8	9.8

ACTIVITY 37

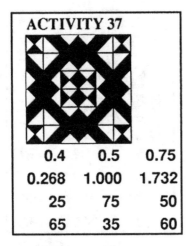

0.4	0.5	0.75
0.268	1.000	1.732
25	75	50
65	35	60

ACTIVITY 38

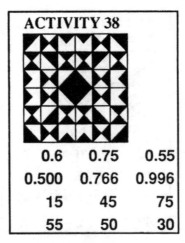

0.6	0.75	0.55
0.500	0.766	0.996
15	45	75
55	50	30

ACTIVITY 39

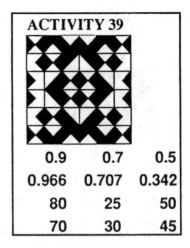

0.9	0.7	0.5
0.966	0.707	0.342
80	25	50
70	30	45

ACTIVITY 40

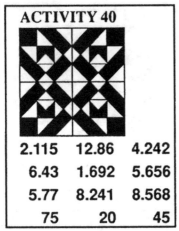

2.115	12.86	4.242
6.43	1.692	5.656
5.77	8.241	8.568
75	20	45

ACTIVITY 41

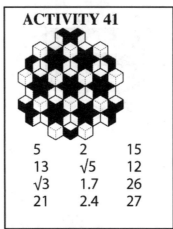

5	2	15
13	$\sqrt{5}$	12
$\sqrt{3}$	1.7	26
21	2.4	27

ACTIVITY 42

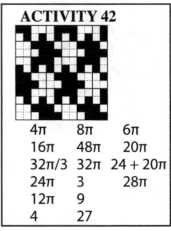

4π	8π	6π
16π	48π	20π
32π/3	32π	24 + 20π
24π	3	28π
12π	9	
4	27	

ACTIVITY 43

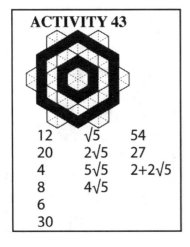

12	$\sqrt{5}$	54
20	$2\sqrt{5}$	27
4	$5\sqrt{5}$	$2+2\sqrt{5}$
8	$4\sqrt{5}$	
6		
30		

ACTIVITY 44

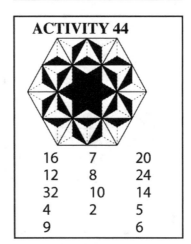

16	7	20
12	8	24
32	10	14
4	2	5
9		6